THE

LITTLE PALM ISLAND

COOKBOOK

THE
LITTLE PALM ISLAND
COOKBOOK

A Tropical Journey

FEATURING RECIPES BY CHEF LUIS POUS

First published in the United States of America by
Hawthorn Creative.

33 Jewell Court
Portsmouth, New Hampshire 03801

Telephone: 603-610-0533

Fax: 603-610-0532

h a w t h o r n c r e a t i v e . c o m

CONTENTS

////////////////////////////////////

FOREWORD

Being totally submerged in the food world and as a chef, there are only a few things that really make me excited to eat and hungry to sink my teeth into. Some of those

things that truly stand out are anything and everything Luis Pous touches. His mastery of Latin and Caribbean cookery truly reigns supreme. Through years of work, struggle, and the fight to survive in Cuba, Luis learned to use whatever he had available to make delicious meals and stand out as an artist when he arrived here in South Florida.

As a chef, he is generous, intelligent, organized, and creative. His food truly tells a tale of what he has been

through and where he is now. Luis uses a harmonious combination of ingredients and classical to modern techniques to make food delicate yet intense, poetic yet approachable.

When you taste his recipes, you will find little gifts and surprises with every bite. He adds hints of sweet and pungent to things most of us would never think of, and just wait until you taste what he can do with a plantain or a piece of fish.

I will forever dream of his foie gras dishes and his perfectly cooked steaks. I always feel lucky when I can take the quick boat over to Little Palm Island so I can enjoy a meal again and again.

There is a certain light richness to his foods, a fingerprint that he puts on his recipes that will make you know for certain that it is a Luis Pous original. His personality and character are truly of his own, and once you get into this book and get down and dirty with these recipes, you will get to know the chef for yourself, something I feel very lucky to have experienced.

Luis is one of the most highly regarded Latin chefs in America, and I am humbled and delighted that he has chosen me to write this for him. I can't wait to get a copy of this book myself so I can finally figure out how he makes the recipes I have been craving for years! *Buen apetito!*

–Michelle Bernstein
iconic Miami chef &
James Beard Award winner

CHEF LUIS POUS, AN INTRODUCTION

To become the chef he is today, Luis Pous left his home in Cuba for an arena that would introduce his palate to the array of world flavors cast throughout the United States. Emigration would also introduce the world to the talents of Luis Pous. It seems ironic, then, that the native habanero's greatest arena, the one that has sent reverberations through the nation's culinary circles, should come from a tiny little island tucked halfway down the necklace of the Florida Keys.

Pous isn't a man of second chances. Just as well, because at his level of gastronomy, there is no room for error. Since arriving on these shores in 1997, he has taken his opportunities and converted. You can see it in the trajectory of his career and taste it in every dish, like the skin on his grilled fish, or the color of the meaty mango he turns toward any number of sweet and savory dishes.

Arriving at Little Palm's kitchen in 2006, Pous took The Dining Room and gave it acclaim with its 2010 *Zagat Survey* distinction as the "Best Hotel Dining" experience in Florida and the third best in the country. The review and ratings guide used "extraordinary to perfection" to laud its food and service, which, in the 42-year-old's lexicon of hospitality, are siamese. In his drive to be, in his words, "the best all-round culinarian," Pous stresses that it is everything from the warm welcome to the absence of up-sell that makes this island dining retreat a natural winner. "The first thing I tell my guests is 'sit down and relax. You are not here to think; we'll do that,'" he explains. "I don't want them to eat with 10 forks. I want them to be comfortable. Here is not like eating at The French Laundry or one of Alain Ducasse's restaurants. To me, the sign of good food is the reaction of my guests when their plates come to the table. Nothing else."

What mattered most growing up in Cuba was survival. "You could be arrested for a piece of food in your hand," recalls Pous, who, at 17, entered the Sergio Perez Government School of the Culinary Arts. Cooking for foreign dignitaries and bona fide communist party members was part and parcel with his culinary education. For the young man, so was grabbing samples of rare foods like caviar for his family to try. As with his cooking, high-risk, high-reward is a personality trait that fits. "My food is Cuban influenced. So it has big flavors," notes Pous. "When chefs say, 'Can you taste that? There is a hint of ginger coming out?' I don't. My food is coming at you. If I use cumin, you'll get cumin. If it's garlic, you'll know it."

It is no surprise that Pous's success has come from the harmony of finding a restaurant in a place that suits his style and temperament. It's the reward from his Huck Finn–esque journey that began in 1997 at the celebrity hot spot The Big Fish restaurant on the Miami River and sent him on to the Renaissance in Atlanta, where he met his mentor and steward, Raymond Saja. He then followed Saja to New York's Hotel Plaza Athénée, where the partnership made it one of the top 50 hotel restaurants in the world as acknowledged by *Condé Nast*. The next few years were spent hopping between Florida and Mississippi, rounding out his resume while moving closer to his home and the food he felt most connected to.

Landing on Little Palm Island, things clicked. Here was where Pous could dazzle with his Latin-yet-straightforward style, putting out light, refreshing flavors to suit the island appetite. Take fish. "I cook fish the best way: in the broiler," says the father of one, who cooked at the James Beard House in 2010. "My direction to my culinary team is to keep it as simple as possible. If they are sautéing the fish…a little

> "WHEN CHEFS SAY, 'CAN YOU TASTE THAT? THERE IS A HINT OF GINGER COMING OUT?' I DON'T. MY FOOD IS COMING AT YOU. IF I USE CUMIN, YOU'LL GET CUMIN. IF IT'S GARLIC, YOU'LL KNOW IT."

butter and tarragon…nothing on the top. On the side, sure, but leave the fish alone."

In his new role as the corporate chef of Noble House, which he rose to in 2012, Pous oversees the food and dining experience at the company's 53 nationwide eateries. Being charged with creating entire menu concepts, setting up new kitchens, instilling "the Pous way" in teams of uninitiated cooks is his charted course coming full circle: "I've

always had a vision of trying to make things work – seeing how everything comes together as a big idea. I don't just see the food." It's another opportunity, one, which despite taking him away from his beloved island, he will transform into another successful entry in his resume. And one that will bear his signature just as much as the indelible dishes that are so clearly his in the pages that follow.

THE DINING ROOM,
LITTLE PALM'S PRIVATE EDEN

While the pompom fronds in the palm trees cheer on morning's arrival and the putt-putt of fishing boats is a ways from stealing the tranquility, preparations for another day

on Little Palm Island have begun. Oranges are squeezed and fresh fruit sliced. Baked goods in the oven are rising with the sun that brings sparkle and color to this island, where relaxation and hospitality are as entwined as the black mangroves and their contortions to grip the land. Guests of the island will soon appear – most, at any rate. Others will opt for their morning meal to be delivered to their rooms because nothing across these five acres of calm is ever rushed. In this land of perpetual summer, the only consideration of speed is how slow you want to go.

At the epicenter of life on Little Palm Island is The Dining Room. If relaxation and pleasure are the hallmarks of a stay here, then eating and drinking are what guests see as fundamental to the entire experience. Resort life revolves around food. In terms of quality and reputation, The Dining Room speaks for itself. And the food speaks to the region, climate, and the Cuban chef who transformed its cuisine into a culinary claxon, turning heads from New York to Los Angeles. Luis Pous took over the restaurant in 2006 as executive chef. In 2010, *Zagat Survey* praised Pous's kitchen as the "Best Hotel Dining in Florida" and third best in the U.S. By the time he left in 2012 to become corporate chef for all Noble House Hotels and Resorts (the management company that oversees operations at Little Palm Island), Pous had installed a culture of exemplary service, attention to detail, and food fit for sonnets. That culture continues through the entire staff and, in particular, the delicate hands and exacting eye of Pastry Chef Dawn Runge, who worked alongside Pous and continues to make sure every finishing bite at The Dining Room is met with a flourish. Pous acknowledges he couldn't have done it without her.

The art of catering to guests' most every request is ingrained. If a guest happens to catch one of the eminently delicious fish roaming the nearby water, the kitchen staff will prepare it. If a returning customer yearns for a dish that is no longer on the menu, again, the kitchen will see to it that his heart's desire is fulfilled. In fact, so far has the reputation of The Dining Room reached that it isn't only Little Palm's self-marooned guests who adore its hospitality, but others come via seaplanes and boats for a night of indelible indulgence. The Dining Room is open to anyone who can reach its shores, and its fans go to great lengths just to pull up a chair.

As noon approaches, lunchtime comes with a variety

IN THIS LAND
OF PERPETUAL
SUMMER, THE ONLY
CONSIDERATION
OF SPEED IS
HOW SLOW YOU
WANT TO GO.

of dining options and adventures to match. Whether by land, sea, or air, foods are packed with guests searching the Keys by seaplane for a priceless picnic spot, casting off for the reefs, or meandering along the beach only to plop down a few feet from their bungalow to eat under the shade of tree. Around the pool, island life is picking up and the fare is casual and light. Composed dishes must wait for the evening's grand affair. The midday meal is simple

with fish tacos or Cuban sandwiches garnering most of the attention. Servers and beach attendants glide through the teak-furnished oasis, serving cooling drinks to the poolsiders or those at the Palapa Bar.

Afternoon is a time for relaxation, massages, walking the island observing the tiny Key Deer that swim over from neighboring islands at low tide, or getting a shot of Spencer, the blue heron that has been around the island for 15 years. It's also a time to return to the comfort of one's accommodation for that snooze or to pick up a book, or just be together…alone. After all, this is one of the most romantic

getaways to be found north of the Equator.

With the sun nearing the horizon, the transformation of The Dining Room is underway and will serve as the epicenter of island life for the next five hours. White linens, crystal stemware, tiki torches, and the tapering clouds now daubed in magenta all come together in stunning concert. Here, the complete dining experience shines in dishes that are featured in magazines like edible pinups and service that is so good it almost isn't there. Formality is served up Florida style, allowing comfort and relaxation to rule. Chef Pous has built a seventh-heaven dining destination where propriety can stay on the mainland.

The events, tastes, sights, and evocations of a single day spent on Little Palm Island remain vivid for most who come to stay. Many return to partake once more in the splendor of guilt-free do-nothing. What follows in these pages are these impressions put to food, described in flavors, and represented in mouthwatering photography. These 36 recipes cover the gamut of The Dining Room's signature dishes – the same recipes that brought it so much recognition. Moreover, what this book and these recipes capture collectively is a sensory arc of a day on the island, forging memories of both food and the island experience that lasts long after guests step foot off *The Truman* back into reality.

On Little Palm Island, dining is the way a fiction writer would have it be. "As I ate the oysters with their strong taste of the sea and their faint metallic taste that the cold white wine washed away… I lost the empty feeling and began to be happy and to make plans," wrote Ernest Hemmingway in his book of memoirs, *A Moveable Feast*, penned not 70 miles from Little Palm in Pous's hometown of Havana. The self-reflection inspired by food and the time taken to enjoy its flavor and effects could well be explained by the combination of hot sun, a sea breeze, and time without routine. It could also be explained right here within a book that has less to do with food than it does about a place of inspiration.

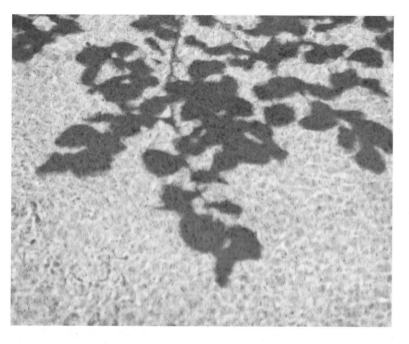

breakfast

//////////////////////////

BRIOCHE FRENCH TOAST

INGREDIENTS

Guava Marmalade
1	c. guava paste
2	c. water
1	vanilla bean
6	tsp. sugar

Almond Mascarpone Cheese
2	c. mascarpone cheese, at room temperature
½	tsp. almond extract
1	c. almonds, toasted

French Toast
12	Texas toast–style slices of bread
24	eggs
8	c. granulated sugar
2	gallons whole milk
1½	c. cinnamon
1½	c. vanilla extract
1	c. Myers's dark rum
1	12-oz. can Coco Lopez or coconut milk
1	18-oz. box cornflakes

PREPARATION

Guava Marmalade
1. Combine all of the ingredients in a pot and simmer until the mixture is syrup consistency (15–20 minutes on medium heat).

Almond Mascarpone Cheese
1. Mix all the ingredients in a mixer on low speed until smooth.

French Toast
1. Portion the brioche into 1 ½-" rounds, place a cooling rack onto a large sheet pan, then lay out the brioche rounds on the rack. Oven-dry the brioche at 225° F for 30 minutes, then remove from the oven and let cool at room temperature for 1 hour.

2. Whisk together the eggs and sugar until smooth, then add the remaining ingredients except the cornflakes and mix until combined.

3. Dunk the dried bread in the mixture for 1 minute on each side then dredge through the crushed corn flakes, making sure the entire outside of the brioche is covered with a layer of cornflakes. Place the coated brioche on a parchment-lined sheet pan.

4. Bake in a preheated oven at 350° F for 15–20 minutes, until warm and crispy.

5. Place a scoop of the mascarpone cheese onto each of the French toast as it comes out of the oven.

Little Palm prefers to have the guava marmalade chilled because of the hot environment and the contrast between hot French toast and chilled marmalade is what makes it; however, the guava sauce can be served warm, as well.

ZERO-FAT EGG WHITE OMELET

//

INGREDIENTS

3   eggs (whites only)
1   tsp. tomato, diced
1   tsp. Spanish onion, diced
2   tsp. spinach, chopped
Salt and pepper to taste

PREPARATION

1. Preheat oven to 400° F. In a mixing bowl, whip the egg whites with a whisk until they are very frothy.

2. Gently fold in the tomato, onion, and spinach.

3. Lightly coat the inside of a 6-ounce ramekin with nonstick spray. Spoon the mixture into the ramekin.

4. Bake until light golden brown (approx. 15–20 minutes). Season with salt and pepper to taste.

//

FLORIDA LOBSTER HASH WITH POACHED EGG, PAPAS BRAVAS & HOLLANDAISE

INGREDIENTS

Hollandaise Sauce
4   eggs (yolks only)
1   tbsp. fresh-squeezed lemon juice
½   c. unsalted clarified butter
Pinch of cayenne pepper
Salt and pepper to taste

Papas Bravas
5   large Idaho potatoes
½   tsp. cayenne pepper
1   tbsp. Spanish paprika
1   bunch parsley, chopped
2   c. mayonnaise
Salt and freshly ground white pepper to taste
Canola oil for frying

Lobster Hash
1   poblano pepper, diced medium
1   red bell pepper, diced one inch
1   red onion, diced one inch
1   tbsp. butter
1   8-oz. Caribbean lobster tail, diced
1   tsp. cilantro, chopped
4   eggs, poached

PREPARATION

Hollandaise Sauce
1. Vigorously whisk the egg yolks and lemon juice together in a stainless-steel bowl until the mixture is thick and double the original volume.

2. Place the bowl over a saucepan containing simmering water. The simmering water should not touch the bottom of the bowl. Continue to whisk rapidly, being careful not to let the eggs get too hot or they will scramble.

3. Slowly drizzle in the clarified butter while whisking until the sauce is thickened and double the volume. Add a tablespoon of warm water to the mixture if it gets too thick.

4. Remove from heat and add the cayenne and salt.

Papas Bravas
1. In a mixing bowl, combine the paprika, cayenne, chopped parsley, and mayo; season well with the salt and pepper. Set aside. This is the Papas Brava sauce.

2. Deep-fry the potatoes in canola oil at 250° F for 15 minutes. Transfer to a sheet pan and cool for 45 minutes.

3. Deep-fry again at 350° F until golden brown (approx. 4–5 minutes).

4. Set aside until ready to serve.

Lobster Hash
1. Sauté the peppers and onions in half of the butter until tender, then move to a medium mixing bowl.

2. Sauté the lobster tail in the remaining butter until it's almost fully cooked (approx. 4–6 minutes) over high heat (stir-fry-style cooking).

3. Add the cooked lobster to the peppers and onions.

4. Add the cooked potatoes to the mixture and add the Papas Brava sauce; mix until combined.

5. Place hash in center of each plate, top with a poached egg and prepared hollandaise. Garnish with cilantro.

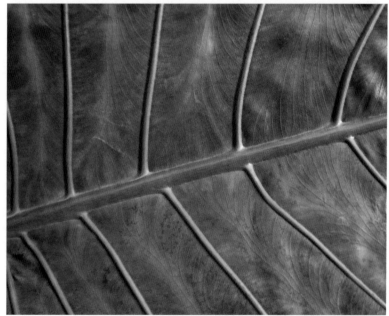

lunch

////////////////////////////////

PLANTAIN-POLENTA FRIES

{SIDE DISH}

//

INGREDIENTS

2	qt. chicken stock
4	green plantains
2	c. instant corn polenta
1	tsp. toasted cumin, slightly ground
2	tbsp. cornmeal for dredging

Vegetable oil for frying

Salt and white pepper to taste

PREPARATION

1. In a large saucepan, heat the chicken stock to a boil.

2. Peel the plantains and put them in a food processor to make a paste. Whisk the plantain paste into the boiling chicken stock.

3. Whisking constantly, add the polenta to the chicken stock a little at a time.

4. Cook the mixture for 8 minutes, then pour it onto a sheet pan and place the pan in the refrigerator to cool. Once cool, turn the pan over and dump the mixture onto a cutting board. Cut the polenta into ½"-long sticks.

5. Dust the sticks with cornmeal and deep-fry.

6. Fry in 375° F vegetable oil until the sticks float and are a light golden brown (approx. 3–5 minutes).

//

KEY WEST SHRIMP FIRE & ICE SALAD

{APPETIZER}

INGREDIENTS

Ponzu Sauce

6	oz. garlic and black bean paste (from specialty store)
½	c. brown sugar
¾	c. rice wine vinegar
¼	c. sesame oil
½	c. light soy sauce
½	c. white sesame seeds, toasted
½	c. black sesame seeds, toasted
1	c. red pepper, diced
½	c. fresh cilantro (stems and all), chopped
½	c. fresh basil, chopped
1½	tbsp. sambal
1	c. sweet chile sauce

Salad

2	c. watermelon, cubed
1	small cucumber, seeded and diced
8	large cooked shrimp, diced
4	c. napa cabbage, shredded
10	cherry tomatoes, halved
½	red onion, sliced

PREPARATION

Ponzu Sauce

1. Mix all of the ingredients together with a whisk.

2. For the best taste, refrigerate overnight.

Salad

1. Toss all of the ingredients with the sauce. The amount of sauce, vegetables, fruit, and shrimp used will be to your liking.

CRAB FRITTERS, CUCUMBER & QUESO FRESCO SALSA, GARLIC AIOLI

{APPETIZER}

INGREDIENTS

Garlic Aioli

⅓ c. garlic cloves
2 tsp. olive oil
1½ c. mayonnaise
⅓ c. fresh-squeezed lemon juice
2 tsp. Italian flat-leaf parsley, chopped
Salt and freshly ground black pepper to taste

Cucumber & Queso Fresco

1 seedless euro cucumber, peeled and diced
1 c. queso fresco, diced small
2 tbsp. extra virgin olive oil
1 tsp. fresh-squeezed lime juice
1 tsp. dried oregano
Salt and pepper to taste

Crab Fritters

1 lb. jumbo lump crabmeat
½ c. mayonnaise
1 tbsp. Dijon mustard
½ c. red onion, diced small
⅓ c. red pepper, diced small
⅓ c. yellow pepper, diced small
1½ c. panko bread crumbs
1 tbsp. lime juice
1 bunch cilantro, chopped
1 egg
Salt and white pepper to taste
Canola oil for frying

PREPARATION

Garlic Aioli

1. Preheat oven to 450° F.

2. Toss the garlic in the olive oil, place the garlic and oil in a shallow pan and cover with foil.

3. Roast for 25 minutes.

4. Puree the garlic and oil in a food processor into a smooth paste.

5. Place the mayonnaise, garlic, parsley, and lemon juice in a mixing bowl. Mix well.

6. Adjust the seasoning with salt and pepper to taste.

7. Store in an air-tight container in the refrigerator until ready to use.

Cucumber & Queso Fresco

1. Mix all ingredients together in a small bowl. Can be served chilled or at room temperature.

Crab Fritters

1. In a large mixing bowl, combine all of the ingredients except ½ a cup of the panko and the canola oil. Fold the ingredients together gently without breaking up the lumps of crab.

2. Chill in refrigerator for 1 hour, then shape into 1-ounce patties and coat each patty with the reserved panko.

3. In a deep pan, heat the canola oil to 375° F. Cook the fritters until golden brown (approx. 1–2 minutes). Drain on paper towels after frying.

4. Arrange the queso fresco on the plate, place the fritters on top with a dollop of aioli on each or in a separate ramekin.

CRAB EMPANADAS WITH CHORIZO TARTAR SAUCE

{APPETIZER}

INGREDIENTS

Chorizo Tartar Sauce

5   oz. Spanish chorizo, diced small

2   large kosher pickles, diced small and drained on paper towels

6   tbsp. capers, chopped

2   shallots, diced small

4   tbsp. fresh-squeezed lemon juice

1   c. mayonnaise

2   tsp. cayenne pepper (or less to taste)

Salt and white pepper to taste

Empanadas

1   c. Spanish onion, finely diced

1   lb. lump crabmeat

10   raw empanadas (Goya brand or any good quality, frozen or fresh)

1   tsp. tomato paste

2½   c. piquillo peppers, finely diced

1½   c. roasted corn

½   c. cilantro, chopped

1   tbsp. ground cumin, toasted

1   tsp. cayenne pepper

2   tbsp. fresh-squeezed lime juice

2   tbsp. olive oil

2   tbsp. all-purpose flour

3   oz. rum (2 shot glasses full)

Egg wash (1 egg beaten with a drop of water to loosen; no seasoning)

PREPARATION

Chorizo Tartar Sauce

1. In a small sauté pan, cook the chorizo on medium heat until it renders out its oil (approx. 2 minutes); drain.

2. In a small bowl, mix together the mayonnaise, rendered chorizo, capers, pickles, and shallots. Stir well, then add the lemon juice, cayenne, and season to taste with salt and pepper. Refrigerate for at least 1 hour before serving.

Empanadas

1. In a large pan over medium heat, sweat the onions until translucent. Add the tomato paste and cook for 1 minute, then add the diced peppers, corn, cilantro, cumin, cayenne, lime juice, crabmeat, olive oil, and flour. Deglaze with the rum and cook for 3–5 minutes.

2. Season the mixture to taste, then transfer it to a large sheet pan to cool.

3. Place 2 ounces of the crab filling on a 4" empanada disk, then brush egg wash along the edges and close the empanada using your fingers or a fork.

4. Fry the empanadas in 375° F oil until golden brown (approx. 2 minutes) or cook them in the oven at the same temperature until golden brown (approx. 10–12 minutes). If using the oven, brush them before baking with olive oil or egg wash to help give them a nice color.

5. Serve the tartar sauce in a ramekin or alongside two empanadas on each plate.

GROUPER CEVICHE WITH PLANTAIN MARIQUITAS

{APPETIZER}

//

INGREDIENTS

Ceviche

1   lb. fresh grouper, ⅜" diced

3   c. fresh-squeezed lime juice

½   red onion, julienned

2   red jalapeños (Fresno peppers), diced

2   green jalapeños, diced

1   tsp. ginger, grated

1   c. cilantro, minced

Fine sea salt to taste

Plantain Mariquitas

2   large green plantains

1   large lime, juiced

Salt and pepper to taste

Vegetable oil for frying

PREPARATION

Ceviche

1. Combine the fish, red onion, jalapeños, ginger, cilantro, and salt. Let the mixture sit for at least 15 minutes.

2. Mix in the lime juice. Let the lime juice "cook" the ceviche for at least 10 minutes and no more than 6 hours before serving.

Plantain Mariquitas

1. Using a mandolin, slice the plantains ⅛" thick in circles or length wise. Soak the slices in cold water and lime juice to stop the oxidation until ready to fry.

2. Deep-fry in 350° F oil until light golden brown (approx. 1 minute).

3. Remove from oil and place on paper towels. Season with salt and pepper and serve alongside the ceviche in a separate bowl/container of your choosing.

//

GAZPACHO

INGREDIENTS

5 roma tomatoes
1 English cucumber, peeled
2 red bell peppers
1 red onion, peeled
8 garlic cloves
2 slices white bread
1 tsp. cayenne pepper
½ c. olive oil
1 c. tomato juice
½ c. red wine vinegar
Salt and pepper to taste

PREPARATION

1. Roughly chop the vegetables, garlic, and bread, then place them in a mixing bowl and season well with the cayenne and salt and pepper.

2. Add the olive oil, tomato juice, and vinegar to the bowl; toss all the ingredients.

3. Transfer the mixture to a large bowl or pitcher and refrigerate overnight.

4. Toss the mixture again and puree it in a blender, working with small batches, until it's very smooth.

5. Pass the soup through a fine chinois and chill well before serving.

CONCH CEVICHE

//

INGREDIENTS

1	lb. conch fillet, sliced against the grain (approx. ⅓" thick)
5	roma tomatoes, diced small
1	bunch cilantro
½	large red onion, diced small
2	poblano peppers, diced small
1	habanero pepper, sliced thin
1	tsp. crushed cumin seed, toasted
⅓	c. olive oil
⅓	c. lime juice

Salt and pepper to taste

PREPARATION

1. In a large mixing bowl, combine the conch, tomato, cilantro, onion, peppers, cumin, salt, and pepper and mix well. Let the mixture sit for 1 hour.

2. Add the olive oil and lime juice. Serve within 1 hour as long as it is chilled well. Like any other ceviche, this dish will be heavy on salt to cut the acidity of the lime. Add more salt to taste.

//

44 | *LUNCH*

COCONUT-CONCH CHOWDER

INGREDIENTS

1   lb. conch, ground

1   qt. tomato juice

1   qt. coconut milk

2   potatoes, peeled and diced

½   c. water

2   tsp. sherry vinegar

2   tsp. cayenne pepper

2   tbsp. fresh-squeezed lime juice

½   c. parsley, finely chopped

2   stalks celery, diced

3   garlic cloves, minced

1   large white onion, peeled and diced

1   large red pepper, seeded and diced

1   large green pepper, seeded and diced

2   bay leaves

⅓   c. blended oil

2   tsp. tomato paste

Salt and pepper to taste

PREPARATION

1. In a large saucepot, combine the celery, garlic, onions, peppers, bay leaves, and blended oil. Slowly sweat the vegetables on medium heat (2–3 minutes), until they become translucent.

2. Add the tomato paste and cook over low heat for 10 minutes, stirring often.

3. Turn the heat up to medium and add the ground conch and tomato juice.

4. Bring the soup to a quick boil, then simmer uncovered for 1 hour.

5. Stir in the coconut milk and potatoes.

6. Simmer (don't let it boil) until the potatoes are tender (approx. 35–45 minutes), then add the water, sherry vinegar, cayenne pepper, and lime juice.

7. Stir well and add the parsley, salt, and pepper to taste.

8. Remove from heat. You can serve immediately, but this dish tastes better the next day. Place the pot in an ice bath, stirring frequently, until cool. Then transfer to a refrigerator overnight. Reheat gently without allowing to boil and serve.

CHICKEN LETTUCE WRAPS
WITH CARIBBEAN SLAW

//

INGREDIENTS

Avocado Ceviche
4   avocados, diced small

4   oz. red onion, diced small

4   oz. tomatoes, diced small

3   oz. cilantro, chopped

6   tbsp. fresh-squeezed lime juice

2   tsp. olive oil

Salt and pepper to taste

Chipotle-Soy Vinaigrette
4   garlic cloves

⅓   c. soy sauce

¼   c. honey

1½   oz. canned chipotle peppers in Adobo

4   tbsp. fresh-squeezed lemon juice

1½   c. vegetable oil

2   oz. cilantro, chopped

Salt and pepper to taste

Caribbean Slaw
1   head cabbage, julienned

1   yellow pepper, julienned

1   red pepper, julienned

1   green pepper, julienned

1   red onion, julienned

6   jalapeños, julienned

1   bunch cilantro, leaves only

½   c. fresh-squeezed lime juice

½   c. Florida orange juice

½   c. white vinegar

1   c. olive oil

2   tbsp. salt

Pinch freshly ground white pepper

Lettuce Wraps
¼   c. molasses

¼   c. soy sauce

1   tbsp. fresh cilantro, chopped

4   boneless chicken thighs

1   head Boston bibb lettuce, separated into individual leaves

PREPARATION

Avocado Ceviche
1. In a medium mixing bowl, combine all the ingredients except the lime juice and cilantro; let stand 5–10 minutes.

2. Add the lime juice and cilantro and toss together. Season to taste with salt and pepper.

Chipotle-Soy Vinaigrette
1. Place the garlic, soy sauce, honey, chipotle peppers, and lemon juice in a blender and puree at medium speed until everything is well incorporated.

2. With the blender running slowly, add the oil to create a smooth sauce consistency.

3. Remove the sauce from the blender and stir in the chopped cilantro. Add salt and pepper to taste.

//

///

Caribbean Slaw

1. Combine all of the ingredients in a mixing bowl and mix thoroughly.

Lettuce Wraps

1. Whisk together the molasses and soy sauce.

2. Add the chopped cilantro.

3. Place the chicken thighs in the molasses/soy/cilantro mixture and refrigerate for up to 2 hours or overnight.

4. Sear the marinated chicken thighs over medium-high heat until browned and cooked through (approx. 4–6 minutes).

5. Let rest for a few minutes before slicing into strips.

6. Present the chicken, lettuce leaves, slaw, avocado ceviche, and vinaigrette separately to allow diners to assemble wraps to their liking.

///

cocktails

////////////////////////////////

GUMBY SLUMBER

//

INGREDIENTS

1½ oz. Captain Morgan spiced rum

1½ oz. Parrot Bay coconut rum

½   oz. orange juice

½   oz. pineapple juice

Splash of cranberry juice

1   tsp. shredded coconut, soaked in
       Bacardi 151 rum

PREPARATION

1. Pour the two types of rum over ice
in a highball glass.

2. Top off with equal amounts of pineapple juice and orange juice.

3. Add a splash of cranberry juice
for color.

4. Rim glass with rum-soaked
coconut.

//

KEY LIME PIE MARTINI

///

INGREDIENTS

Simple Syrup

1   c. sugar

½   c. hot water

This is amounts for 1 serving. If producing a larger batch, use 2 parts sugar to 1 part water.

Martini

2   oz. Bacardi Limon

½   oz. (⅓ shot glass full) Liquor 43 (vanilla-flavored liquor)

1   small scoop vanilla ice cream, melted

1   tbsp. lime juice

Lime slice for garnish

Graham cracker crumbs for garnish

PREPARATION

Simple Syrup

1. Bring water to boil and add sugar until completely dissolved.

2. Remove from heat, and let cool.

Martini

1. Garnish the rim of a martini glass with graham cracker crumbs.

2. Combine the liquor, melted ice cream, lime juice, and simple syrup in a cocktail shaker with ice. Shake vigorously and strain the drink into the martini glass. Garnish with a slice of lime.

///

SER
VES

1

WATERMELON & JALAPEÑO MOJITO

///

INGREDIENTS

1½ oz. Bacardi Limon

5   fresh mint leaves

2–3 cubes fresh watermelon

2   slices of jalapeño

1   oz. fresh-squeezed lime juice

1   oz. simple syrup (see Key Lime
      Pie Martini recipe for instruc-
      tions, p. 53)

Splash of soda water

Lime garnish

PREPARATION

1. Muddle the mint leaves, watermelon cubes, and slices of jalapeño with 1 ounce simple syrup.

2. Add rum and lime juice.

3. Shake with ice. Pour mixture in glass and top with a splash of soda water.

4. Garnish with a wedge of lime.

///

JAMAICAN ME KRAZY

//

INGREDIENTS

1½ oz. Bacardi Limon
2 oz. mango puree
1 oz. raspberry puree
Orange slice for garnish

PREPARATION

1. Blend Bacardi Limon, mango puree, and a scoop of ice.

2. Pour mixture over raspberry puree.

3. Garnish with orange.

//

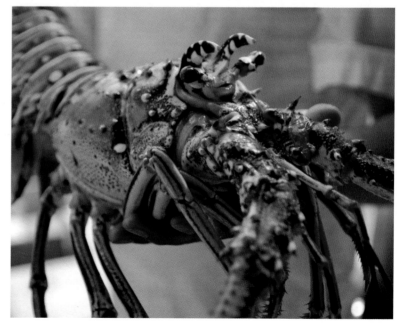

dinner

///////////////////////////////

SER
VES

8

MUSHROOM CEVICHE

{SIDE DISH}

//

INGREDIENTS

2	qt. shiitake mushrooms, quartered
¼	c. ginger, minced
1	c. red onion, fine julienned
½	qt. fresh-squeezed lime juice, salted (1 tbsp. kosher salt)
½	c. red jalapeños, fine julienned
1½	c. snow peas, fine julienned (tips removed)
1	c. scallions, cut thin on the bias

Salt and pepper to taste

PREPARATION

1. In a mixing bowl, combine the mushrooms, ginger, red onion, and lime juice. Depending on how firm you prefer the mushrooms, this dish can be served right away for a firmer texture or refrigerated overnight for a softer texture.

2. Just before serving, add the remaining ingredients and re-season to taste.

//

JALAPEÑO CORNBREAD

{SIDE DISH}

///

INGREDIENTS

½   lb. all-purpose flour

½   lb. cornmeal

¼   c. sugar

1   tsp. baking powder

1   tsp. salt

2   eggs

2   c. milk

½   sticks butter, melted

1   c. pepper jack cheese, shredded

1   jalapeño, finely chopped

½   c. roasted red pepper,
    finely chopped

PREPARATION

1. Preheat oven to 350° F. Mix the ingredients together, then pour into an 8" square baking pan.

2. Bake the cornbread in a 350° F oven for 50–60 minutes. The top should be a light golden brown and a toothpick should come out clean after being inserted into the middle.

///

SER
VES

6

TUNA & FOIE GRAS CEVICHE

{APPETIZER}

//

INGREDIENTS

½   c. orange juice

1   tsp. sesame oil

2   tsp. rice wine vinegar

2   limes, juiced

2   tsp. hot sauce

18 oz. blackfin tuna, diced

¼   c. red onion, julienned

2   segments Florida orange

¼   c. cilantro leaves

6   oz. Hudson Valley foie gras

1   Asian pear, julienned

1   c. micro herb salad

Salt and pepper to taste

PREPARATION

1. In a mixing bowl, combine the orange juice, sesame oil, rice wine vinegar, lime juice, and hot sauce. Mix the vinaigrette with a fork or whisk, and set aside.

2. In a separate mixing bowl, combine the tuna, red onion, orange segments, and cilantro, and set aside for at least 20 minutes. Then, add the vinaigrette to the tuna mixture, reserving a small amount to lightly dress the micro greens. Season to taste with salt and pepper.

3. Season the foie gras heavily with salt and pepper and cook it on a very hot sauté pan for about 1 minute on each side, until golden brown. Let the foie gras cool, then cut it in cubes.

4. To serve, place the ceviche in the middle of the plate. Top the ceviche with the foie gras and micro greens; assort the julienned Asian pear on the plate. Drizzle the remaining vinaigrette over the greens and pear.

//

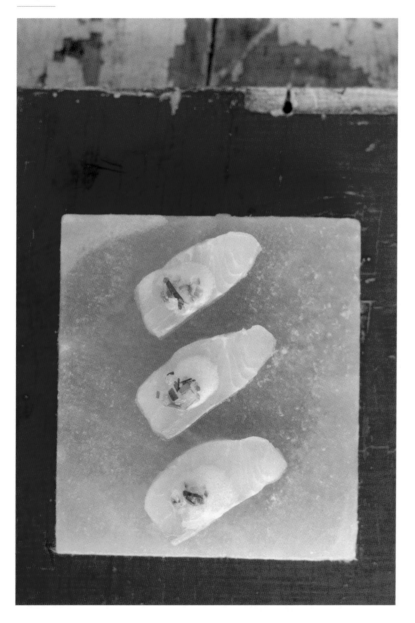

FLORIDA SWORDFISH TIRADITO WITH MOJO AMARILLO

{APPETIZER}

INGREDIENTS

1 lb. sushi-grade or super fresh swordfish fillet

½ lb. aji amarillo peppers, seeded

½ c. white vinegar

1 head garlic, cleaned and smashed

¾ c. fresh-squeezed lime juice

6 oz. queso fresco

1½ c. vegetable oil

Salt to taste

PREPARATION

1. With your sharpest knife, cut the swordfish into a 2" x 2" x 4" block. Starting with the part of the knife edge closest to the handle and then drawing it back toward you in one smooth motion (do not saw it), cut the meat against the grain into thin slices about ⅓" thick. Set aside.

2. In a blender, combine all other ingredients except the vegetable oil. Start blending on low and gradually increase to high speed. When the mixture is smooth, slowly add the vegetable oil while blending.

3. Taste the mixture and season with salt to taste. Keep in mind the lime juice is key in this sauce. When you taste, if it's too tart, add a little more oil, but if the taste is little dull, add a little more lime juice.

4. Place the slices of swordfish on the plate, then drizzle the sauce on top.

SER
VES

6

FOIE GRAS CUBAN SANDWICH WITH BANANA TENTACIÓN

{APPETIZER}

INGREDIENTS

Banana Tentación
1 c. sugar
1 c. white wine
2 cinnamon sticks
2 bananas, fully ripened

Jalapeño Pesto
1 c. firmly packed fresh basil
2 tbsp. firmly packed cilantro
1 clove garlic
½ tsp. roasted garlic paste
1 roasted jalapeño, peeled and seeded
¼ c. Spanish peanuts, toasted
¼ c. Parmesan cheese, grated
¼ c. manchego cheese, grated
½ c. extra virgin olive oil
Salt and pepper to taste

Sandwich
1 750-ml bottle sherry wine
9 oz. foie gras, grade A (cut into 1½ oz. pieces, 1" thick)
6 tbsp. jalapeño pesto (above recipe)
3 oz. serrano ham, sliced (6 slices)
3 oz. manchego cheese, sliced (6 slices)
1 loaf Cuban bread

PREPARATION

Banana Tentación
1. Preheat oven to 375° F.

2. In a small oven-proof saucepan, combine the sugar, wine, and cinnamon sticks. Bring the mixture to a boil and reduce the heat to a low simmer. Cook for 15 minutes. Remove from heat.

3. Slice the bananas in half lengthwise. Submerge the banana halves in the syrup in the oven-proof sauce pan. Broil on high heat until golden brown (approx. 8–10 minutes). The bananas should be slightly soft but not mushy.

Jalapeño Pesto
1. Pulse the jalapeño, basil, cilantro, garlic, and roasted garlic paste in a food processor until chopped.

2. Add the peanuts and cheeses and pulse until just blended.

3. While the machine is running, add the olive oil until a uniform consistency is achieved.

4. Season with salt and pepper and set aside until ready to use.

Sandwich
1. Reduce the sherry wine at a low simmer until it's a light syrup (approx. 45–60 minutes) and set aside.

2. Toast the Cuban bread, and spread the jalapeño pesto on the bottom half. Place the serrano ham on top of the pesto.

3. Sear the foie gras in a hot cast-iron skillet on high heat. Place the foie gras on top of the serrano ham and the manchego cheese on top of the foie gras.

4. Place one hot Banana Tentación on the cheese, and drizzle the sherry reduction on it. Place the other slice of bread on top.

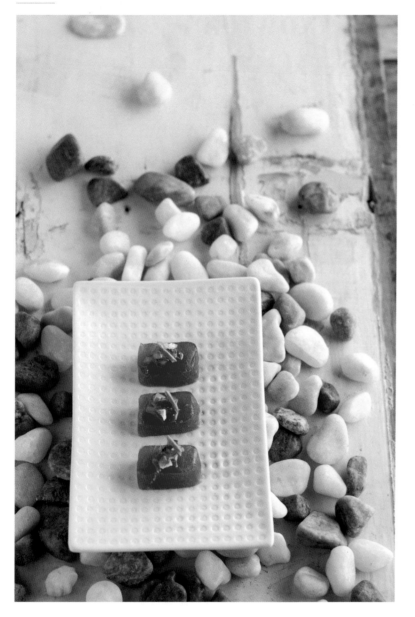

CITRUS-TEQUILA-CURED TUNA

{APPETIZER}

//

INGREDIENTS

1	lb. tuna fillet, skin and bones removed
2	tbsp. lime zest
2	tbsp. orange zest
2	tbsp. lemon zest
2	tbsp. coriander seeds
4	c. salt
4	c. sugar
1	c. citrus-flavored tequila

PREPARATION

1. In a mixing bowl, combine the citrus zests, coriander seeds, salt, and sugar, and mix well.

2. Put half of the mixture in a 2"-deep rectangular stainless-steel pan. Place the tuna on top of the citrus zest mixture, then cover the tuna with the remaining half of the mixture.

3. Pour the tequila on top of the tuna. Let the tuna cure for 3 hours, rinse, and serve. Garnish with sea salt, lemon zest, orange zest, and chives.

//

A TROPICAL JOURNEY

GUAVA BBQ BROILED OYSTERS

{APPETIZER}

INGREDIENTS

Barbecue Sauce

1   tbsp. olive oil

¼   large red onion, finely chopped

2   cloves garlic, minced

1½   c. ketchup

6   oz. guava paste

¼   c. sherry vinegar (or white
       wine vinegar)

2   tbsp. Worcestershire sauce

Water to thin, if necessary

Oysters

12   oysters on the half shell,
       preferably large

3   strips of smoked bacon, cooked
       and chopped fine

1   c. rock salt for presentation

PREPARATION

Barbecue Sauce

1. Heat a sauce pan over medium heat. Once hot, sauté onions in the oil until soft (about 5 minutes). Add garlic and sauté for another minute.

2. Add the remaining ingredients and bring to a gentle simmer, then reduce heat to low. Cover and simmer for 20–30 minutes.

3. Remove from heat and let cool.

4. Blend the mixture at medium speed until smooth consistency. Add water if too thick. Set aside. The sauce can be stored in an air-tight container for up to one month in the refrigerator.

Oysters

1. Preheat broiler on high; place oysters in their shells on large rimmed baking sheet.

2. Add a teaspoon of guava barbecue sauce over each, making sure the entire oyster is covered.

3. Broil until they are caramelized (approx. 3–4 minutes).

4. Transfer oysters in shells onto plates spread with a layer of rock salt. Sprinkle with crispy bacon and serve.

MARINATED CUBAN PORK SHANK & ONION MOJO

///

INGREDIENTS

Mojo Criollo (pork marinade)
1   c. orange juice*
1   c. lime juice*
½   c. Spanish onions, diced
½   c. garlic, chopped
2   tsp. salt
2   tsp. dried oregano
½   c. parsley, chopped
1   tsp. cumin, toasted

Onion Mojo
9   Spanish onions, julienned
2   c. white vinegar
1   qt. blended olive oil for frying
2   bay leaves
Salt and pepper to taste

Cuban Pork Shank
4   pork shanks, skin on
½   tbsp. ground cumin
2   tbsp. fresh-squeezed lime juice
2   tbsp. fresh-squeezed orange juice
1   sprig fresh thyme
1   tbsp. salt
1   tsp. freshly ground black pepper

PREPARATION

Mojo Criollo
1. Mix all of the ingredients together and chill the mixture in the refrigerator overnight before serving.

Onion Mojo
1. Place the onions and bay leaves in a 6"-deep full-size hotel pan.

2. Pour the vinegar into a pot and bring to a simmer; reduce by half (approx. 30 minutes).

3. Pour the oil into a separate pot and heat to 400° F.

4. Pour the hot vinegar over the julienned onions.

5. Immediately pour the hot oil over the onions and let cool (approx. 30 minutes).

6. Let cool completely. Can be served cold, room temperature, or warm.

Pork Shank
1. Preheat oven to 275° F. In a mixing bowl, combine the cumin, juices, thyme, salt, and pepper.

2. Rub the seasoning under the skin; rub the pork shanks with the Mojo Criollo marinade.

3. Marinate overnight in the refrigerator.

4. Place the shanks in a roasting pan and add 2 cups of water to the bottom of the pan.

5. Cover the pan with aluminum foil and place in the preheated oven.

6. Slow roast for six hours, checking periodically and adding water as it evaporates.

7. Remove the cover and raise the temperature to 425° F; watch closely as the skin will get crispy quickly.

8. Once crispy, remove from oven and serve, placing the Onion Mojo alongside the pork shank.

At Little Palm Island, we use sour oranges in this recipe, but sour oranges are hard to find. Instead, you can use the same amount of orange juice and lime juice to get the sour taste.

///

BROILED YELLOWTAIL SNAPPER, PERUVIAN POTATOES, VEGETABLE ESCABECHE & PARSLEY JUS

INGREDIENTS

Parsley Jus
4   bunches of parsley, rough chopped

1   tbsp. salt

2   tbsp. vegetable oil

2   qt. ice water

Vegetable Escabeche
2   carrots, fine julienned

2   red peppers, fine julienned

2   Spanish onions, fine julienned

2   bay leaves

1   c. white vinegar

1   c. blended olive oil for frying

Salt and white pepper to taste

Peruvian Blue Potato Puree
8   medium-sized purple potatoes, peeled

½   lb. butter

1   c. coconut milk

4   tbsp. fresh-squeezed lemon juice

1   tsp. kosher salt

Freshly ground white pepper to taste

Yellowtail Snapper
6   8–10 oz. yellowtail snapper fillets

1   tsp. kosher salt

1   tsp. black pepper

3   tbsp. butter

PREPARATION

Parsley Jus
1. Cook the parsley in a very hot pot on high; add oil and salt.

2. Stir fast until parsley is bright green.

3. Shock in ice water and strain; make sure there are no ice blocks included.

4. Put the parsley into a blender and add 2–3 oz. of the ice water previously used. Blend on high until pureed.

5. Strain through a chinois. Set aside in the refrigerator.

Vegetable Escabeche
1. Put all of the vegetables and the bay leaves in a very deep pan (like a soup pot) and set aside.

2. In a saucepan, heat the white vinegar to a simmer for 10 minutes.

3. In a separate saucepan, bring the oil to 400° F on high.

4. Pour the vinegar over the vegetables that have been set aside in the deep pan. Then, very carefully, pour the oil over the vegetables. Let the mixture cool to room temperature (approx. 1–2 hours). Place in a container to store in the refrigerator or use the same day at room temperature. The escabeche will last for weeks in the refrigerator.

Purple Peruvian Potatoes
1. Put the potatoes in a large pot with just enough water to cover them. Add half of the kosher salt and cook over high heat until the potatoes are tender (approx. 15 minutes).

2. Drain the potatoes and cool. Mash using your method of choice (Pous prefers a potato ricer).

3. Stir in the butter and coconut milk. Season to taste with the ground white pepper and remaining salt.

4. Add lemon juice to enhance flavor and brighten color.

Yellowtail Snapper

1. Preheat oven broiler to 375° F (if your broiler doesn't have temperature options, place it on high).

2. Season the fillets with kosher salt, freshly ground white pepper, and rub with butter.

3. Place on a sheet pan, skillet, or sizzle platter under the broiler for 6–7 minutes. This thin fish will cook through at high heat so no need to flip.

4. Plate the fish on top of the potatoes, then use tongs to place the escabeche on top. Drizzle the Parsley Jus on the plate.

PARMESAN-EGGPLANT SOUP

//

INGREDIENTS

2	tbsp. canola oil
1	large Spanish onion, rough cut
5	large eggplants, rough cut
½	lb. unsalted butter
1	c. shredded Parmesan cheese

Salt and white pepper to taste

PREPARATION

1. Put the canola oil and onions in a stockpot and sweat the onions until translucent on medium heat (approx. 4–6 minutes). Add the eggplant and the butter.

2. Cover the pot and turn the heat down to low. Cook for 1 hour, then remove from heat.

3. Add the contents of the pot to a blender a little at a time, blending for at least 2 minutes each time until smooth. Add the Parmesan cheese and blend well. Season well with salt and white pepper. If the soup gets too thick, add 2–4 oz. water to the blender to your preferred thickness.

//

PARMESAN-ZUCCHINI SOUP

//

INGREDIENTS

2   tbsp. canola oil

1   large Spanish onion, rough cut

6   large zucchini, rough cut

½   lb. unsalted butter

1   c. shredded Parmesan cheese

Salt and white pepper to taste

PREPARATION

1. Put the canola oil and onions in a stockpot and sweat the onions until translucent on medium heat (approx. 4–6 minutes). Add the zucchini and the butter.

2. Cover the pot and turn the heat down to low. Cook for 1 hour, then remove from heat.

3. Add the contents of the pot to a blender a little at a time, blending for at least 2 minutes each time until smooth. Add the Parmesan cheese and blend well. Season well with salt and white pepper. If the soup gets too thick, add 2–4 oz. water to the blender to your preferred thickness.

//

SEARED GROUPER WITH AVOCADO-POBLANO PEPPER SAUCE & ORANGE-ONION MOJO

INGREDIENTS

Paprika Oil
1 tbsp. Spanish smoked paprika
1 c. canola oil
Pinch salt

Avocado-Poblano Pepper Sauce
2 avocados
2 poblano peppers, roasted and peeled
½ c. water
½ c. lime juice
1 c. queso fresco
1 tbsp. sour cream
Pinch salt
Pinch white pepper

Orange-Onion Mojo
9 Spanish onions, fine julienned
2 c. white vinegar
1 qt. blended oil
2 bay leaves
Segments of 2 oranges
Salt and pepper to taste

Grouper
6–7 oz. grouper fillet, skinless
2 tbsp. butter
Kosher salt and freshly ground white pepper to taste

PREPARATION

Paprika Oil
1. Combine the ingredients in a small pot and simmer over low heat for 20 minutes.

2. Strain the oil and cool to room temperature (approx. 1 hour).

Avocado-Poblano-Pepper Sauce
1. Combine all of the ingredients in a food processor and mix until the sauce has a nice puree texture.

Orange-Onion Mojo
1. Place both the onions and the bay leaves in a large casserole pan. Pour the vinegar into a pot. Bring to a simmer and reduce by half (approx. 30–45 minutes).

2. Place the oil into a separate pot and heat to 400° F.

3. Pour the hot vinegar over the onions. Immediately after, pour the hot oil over the onions.

4. Add the orange segments after 5 minutes. Cool for 1 hour and store in containers for later use.

Grouper
1. Preheat oven to 375° F. Season grouper fillets with kosher salt and freshly ground white pepper.

2. Heat two large cast-iron skillets on medium-high heat with blended oil, until smoking hot. Add grouper fillets; cook until golden brown (approx. 2 minutes).

3. Flip the fish, add a tablespoon of butter to each skillet, and place the pans in the oven for 7–8 minutes. Check frequently; cook time will vary depending on thickness of the fish.

4. Spoon sauce evenly onto the center of six plates, top each with a grouper fillet and the mojo. Drizzle each plate with Paprika Oil.

84 | *DINNER*

FIRE-ROASTED RIB EYE WITH PAPAS BRAVAS & CHIMICHURRI

INGREDIENTS

Chimichurri

2   bunches parsley, chopped

¼   c. dried oregano

1   tsp. pepper flakes

¼   c. garlic, chopped

½   c. aged red wine vinegar

1½   c. blended oil

Salt and fresh white pepper to taste

Papas Bravas

5   large Idaho potatoes

½   tsp. cayenne pepper

1   tbsp. Spanish paprika

1   bunch parsley, chopped

2   c. mayonnaise

Salt and pepper to taste

Canola oil for frying

Rib Eye

6   10-oz. rib eye steaks (1¼" thick)

2   tbsp. canola oil

Kosher salt and freshly ground pepper to taste

Pinch of rock salt or fleur du sel for finishing

PREPARATION

Chimichurri

1. Chop the parsley by hand and put it into a mixing bowl with remaining ingredients. The chimichurri develops flavor over time, so is best served in a few hours or the next day. Cover in the refrigerator overnight for best flavor.

Papas Bravas

1. In a mixing bowl, combine the paprika, cayenne, chopped parsley, and mayonnaise. Mix together and season well with the salt and fresh white pepper. Set aside.

2. Deep-fry the potatoes in canola oil at 250° F for 15 minutes, transfer to a sheet pan, and cool.

3. Deep-fry again at 350° F until potatoes are golden brown (approx. 4–5 minutes). Take out and put in a mixing bowl and mix with the cayenne pepper mayonnaise.

Rib Eye

1. Preheat oven to 375° F. Remove steaks from the refrigerator 20–30 minutes before cooking. Season them on both sides with kosher salt and freshly ground black pepper.

2. Heat two large cast-iron skillets with a tablespoon of canola oil in each.

3. Place steaks and sear on one side until the edges become golden brown (approx. 1 ½–2 minutes). Avoid moving the steaks to ensure a perfect sear.

4. Flip steaks and add one tablespoon of butter, cook for another 2 minutes. Again, do not move the steaks. Finish in oven at 375° F for 9-10 minutes for medium rare or 130–140° F internal reading on a meat thermometer.

5. Transfer to a cutting board or cooling rack and let the meat rest for 5–7 minutes. Finish with rock salt or fleur du sel. Plate the Papas Bravas alongside the steak, with the Chimichurri in an accompanying ramekin.

FIRE-ROASTED FILET MIGNON WITH YUCCA GRATIN & MUSHROOM-TRUFFLE CHIMICHURRI

INGREDIENTS

Chimichurri
1½ c. button mushrooms
1½ c. shiitake mushrooms
2   bunches parsley
¼   c. dried oregano
1   tsp. pepper flakes
¼   c. garlic, chopped
½   c. aged red wine vinegar
½   c. white truffle oil
1½   c. blended oil
Salt and fresh white pepper to taste

Gratin
8   yucca, peeled and sliced
1   qt. cream
½   qt. half-and-half
1   tbsp. fresh thyme, stems removed
1   lb. grated manchego cheese
Salt and white pepper to taste

Filet Mignon
6   8 oz. filet mignon
2   tbsp. canola oil
4   tbsp. unsalted butter
Pinch of rock salt or fleur de sel for finishing
Salt and pepper to taste

PREPARATION

Chimichurri
1. Chop the mushrooms in a food processor into small pieces.

2. Chop the parsley by hand and mix in a mixing bowl with all of the other ingredients. The chimichurri develops flavor over time, so it is best served in a few hours or the next day. Keep covered in the refrigerator for best flavor.

Gratin
1. Preheat oven to 350° F. Boil the yucca until tender but still slightly al dente (approx. 20–25 minutes). Drain and let cool.

2. Put the cream, half-and-half, thyme, salt, and pepper in a bowl and mix well.

3. Butter a 2"-deep glass, nonstick, or ceramic cake pan (approx. 12" x 8" or similar).

4. Lay parchment paper on the bottom. Butter the parchment paper.

5. Put a little of the mix in the pan, enough to cover the bottom of the pan, add an even layer of the yucca, and sprinkle grated manchego cheese on top. Repeat the procedure until the pan is full.

6. Cover the pan with aluminum foil and place in a 350° F oven for 2 hours.

Filet Mignon
1. Preheat oven to 375° F. Remove filets from the refrigerator 20–30 minutes before cooking. Season on both sides with kosher salt and freshly ground black pepper.

2. Preheat two large cast-iron skillets with one tablespoon of canola oil in each.

3. Place steaks in skillet and sear on one side until the edges become golden brown (approx. 2–3 minutes), being careful not to move the steaks to ensure the proper sear.

4. Flip steaks and add two tablespoons of butter in each skillet, cook for another 2 minutes. Again, do not move the steaks. Finish in oven at 375° F for 10–12 minutes for medium rare or 130°–140° F internal reading on meat thermometer.

5. Transfer to a cutting board or cooling rack and let the meat rest for 5–7 minutes. Finish with rock salt or fleur du sel.

6. Place steaks on plate with a scoop of the gratin and sauce served in a ramekin.

LOBSTER WITH ROASTED CORN & APPLE RISOTTO

///

INGREDIENTS

Corn Broth

1   qt. water

4   corn cobs (kernels removed and kept for use in finished risotto)

1   tbsp. salt

1   bay leaf

3   sprigs fresh thyme

Corn Risotto

1   c. corn kernels (from cobs used in broth preparation)

¼   c. extra virgin olive oil

1   small yellow onion, finely diced

3   garlic cloves, minced

2   c. Arborio rice

6   c. chicken broth

2   c. prepared corn broth

½   c. dry white wine

½   c. granny smith apple, peeled and diced

½   c. mascarpone cheese

½   c. Parmesan cheese, grated

2   tbsp. butter

1   tbsp. truffle oil

Lobster

2   1½-lb. Maine lobsters, steamed, cooled, meat removed from shells, tails split in half

¼   c. extra virgin olive oil

1   tsp. fresh-squeezed lime juice

1   bay leaf

¼   lb. unsalted butter

Salt and freshly ground black pepper to taste

Plating

½   c. fresh fennel bulb, shaved on a mandolin

1   tsp. extra virgin olive oil

2   tbsp. fresh chives, snipped

PREPARATION

Corn Broth

1. Combine the water, corn cobs, salt, bay leaf, and thyme in a large saucepan and simmer; reduce by half (approx. 20–30 minutes).

2. Adjust the seasoning and strain through a fine mesh strainer. Set aside.

Corn Risotto

1. In a sauté pan, dry roast the corn over medium heat until it begins to char slightly. Remove and set aside.

2. Combine the two broths in a saucepan and bring to a simmer.

3. In a separate large sauce pan, add the oil and then sweat the onion and garlic until fragrant.

4. Add the rice to the pan and stir until all the kernels are coated with oil.

5. Add the wine and continue stirring until it all evaporates.

6. Add 1 cup of the hot combined broths and continue stirring over medium-high heat.

7. When the broth has been absorbed (approx. 5 minutes), add another cup of broth and repeat this process, only adding 1 cup of broth at a time.

8. When the rice is cooked (al dente), add the roasted corn and apples; stir.

///

9. Fold in the mascarpone, Parmesan, butter, and truffle oil, and adjust seasoning to taste.

Lobster

1. Place the lobster meat in a mixing bowl and drizzle with oil and lime juice.

2. Season with salt and pepper and then place in shallow sauté pan.

3. Add the bay leaf, butter, and enough water to cover the lobsters. Gently reheat over low to medium heat (approx. 5 minutes). Remove from the heat and set aside.

Plating

1. Toss the shaved fennel with the oil and season to taste.

2. Divide the finished risotto into 4 serving bowls.

3 Top each with a warm half lobster tail and meat from one claw.

4. Top each plate with shaved fennel and snipped chives.

dessert

///////////////////////////

92 | *DESSERT*

BUÑUELOS DE PASCUA ("HOLIDAY BEIGNETS")

INGREDIENTS

Syrup

½ c. water

1 c. sugar

1 cinnamon stick

2 tbsp. fresh-squeezed lime juice

1 pinch anise seed, ground

1 tsp. white wine

Beignets

2 medium yucca fruits

½ tsp. vanilla extract

½ c. flour

1 egg

Water to loosen batter, if necessary

Pinch of salt

PREPARATION

Syrup

1. In a saucepan, combine all ingredients. Bring to a simmer, stirring until the sugar has melted, then cooked on medium heat until lightly golden brown (approx. 12–15 minutes).

2. Remove from heat and remove the cinnamon stick.

Beignets

1. Peel and dice the yucca and boil in water until tender.

2. Drain and puree the yucca like you would mashed potatoes.

3. On a work surface, knead together the yucca, vanilla, flour, salt, and egg. Knead in enough water to make a soft dough that is smooth and can be piped out of a pastry bag.

4. Put the dough in a piping bag and make into figure eights with 2–3 ounces of dough. Deep-fry the beignets at 350° F until golden brown (approx. 3 minutes).

5. After the beignets are fried, dip them in the spiced-wine syrup and serve.

CHOCOLATE TRUFFLE COOKIES

//

INGREDIENTS

1½ lb. dark chocolate, 60%

½ pound butter

2¾ c. all-purpose flour

⅓ c. dark cocoa powder

2 tsp. baking powder

2 tsp. salt

8 large eggs

1 lb. sugar

1 oz. amaretto, Kahlua, or rum (your preference)

PREPARATION

1. Preheat oven to 325° F. Melt the chocolate and butter together in a saucepan over low heat.

2. In a mixing bowl, sift the flour, cocoa powder, baking powder, and salt together.

3. In a separate mixing bowl, whip the eggs, sugar, and liquor to a thick ribbon.

4. Stir the melted chocolate and butter into the egg mixture, then fold in the flour mixture until it's just combined.

5. Scoop round tablespoons of the dough onto parchment-lined baking sheets and bake at 325° F for 10–15 minutes, just until set. Let the cookies completely cool before removing from baking sheets.

//

COCONUT FLAN

//

INGREDIENTS

2   c. sugar
5   large eggs
1   c. heavy cream
1   tsp. vanilla extract
1   c. coconut milk

PREPARATION

1. Preheat oven to 325° F. In a sauce-pan over medium heat, caramelize 1 ½ cups of the sugar until it is light golden brown, then pour 1 tablespoon of the caramel into each of 4, 6–8 oz. ramekins.

2. Whisk together the eggs, cream, remaining ½ cup of sugar, vanilla, and milk, and pour the mixture into the ramekins over the caramel.

3. Bake the flan in a hot water bath at 325° F for 20–30 minutes, until it is just set. Cool completely before serving.

//

KEY LIME PIE

//

INGREDIENTS

Crust

2   c. roasted, unsalted cashew nuts, finely chopped

¾   c. unsalted butter, melted

1   c. graham cracker crumbs

½   c. granulated sugar

Filling

4   c. sweetened condensed milk

1½ c. key lime juice

12 eggs (yolks only)

Whipped cream for finishing

PREPARATION

Crust

1. Preheat oven to 350° F. Combine all ingredients together in a mixing bowl.

2. Pat firm in a greased 9" cheesecake pan.

3. Bake for 10 minutes.

Filling

1. Add condensed milk to lightly beaten egg yolks.

2. Slowly stir in key lime juice until smooth. Pour over crust.

3. Bake for 20–25 minutes or until set.

4. Chill completely in refrigerator (preferably overnight) before topping with whipped cream.

//

MANGO-GUAVA CHEESECAKE

INGREDIENTS

Oatmeal-Rum "Cookie" Crust
- ½ c. sugar
- ⅓ c. brown sugar
- ½ c. quick oats
- ¼ c. coconut
- ¼ c. butter
- 1 egg (yolk only)
- 2 tbsp. dark rum
- ¼ c. flour
- ⅛ tsp. baking powder
- Pinch of salt
- Pinch of cinnamon

Cheesecake Filling
- 20 oz. cream cheese
- 1½ c. sugar
- 1 tsp. Mexican vanilla
- ½ tsp. salt
- 4 tbsp. fresh-squeezed lemon juice
- 7 eggs
- 1 c. guava marmalade
- 1 c. mango puree

PREPARATION

Oatmeal-Rum "Cookie" Crust

1. In a 350° F oven, toast the oats and coconut on a baking sheet until light golden brown (approx. 10–15 minutes).

2. Cream the butter and sugars together until light and fluffy. Add the egg yolk, rum, baking powder, salt, and cinnamon. Mix until smooth.

3. Stir in the oats, coconut, and flour to combine evenly.

4. Pat the dough into the bottom of a greased 9" cheese pan.

5. Bake in 350° F oven until light golden brown (approx. 12–15 minutes).

Cheesecake Filling

1. In a stand mixer with a paddle attachment, beat the cream cheese with the sugar, vanilla, salt, and lemon juice until smooth, scraping down bowl often.

2. Add all of the eggs, but just the yolks of 3 of them. Blend until smooth.

3. Divide the batter in half in two bowls.

4. Stir the guava marmalade into one half and mango puree into the other half.

5. Pour the guava cheesecake mix over the crust in the cheesecake pan.

6. Pour the mango cheesecake mix into a 9" baking dish. (Neither pan will be full.)

7. Bake both cakes in a 325° F oven for 30–40 minutes or until set. If cakes start to brown before setting, turn oven down to 300° F.

8. Place both cakes in cooler for at least 1 hour to chill completely.

9. In a stand mixer with a whip attachment, whip the chilled mango cheesecake until light and fluffy. Spread evenly over the guava cheesecake and chill for another hour to reset the mango cheesecake.

10. When set, run a wet knife along the side of the mango cheesecake to loosen from the pan and unmold the pan side.